White As a Seashell

Blanco como una concha marina

written by **Molly Dingles**

illustrated by **Walter Velez**

dingles&company New Jersey

First printing

PUBLISHED BY dingles&company
P.O. Box 508 • Sea Girt, New Jersey • 08750
WEBSITE: www.dingles.com • E-MAIL: info@dingles.com

Library of Congress Catalog Card No.: 2004091478
ISBN: 1-891997-38-6

Printed in the United States of America

ART DIRECTED & DESIGNED BY Barbie Lambert

DESIGN ASSISTANT Erin Collity

ENGLISH EDITED BY Andrea Curley SPANISH EDITED BY John Page

EDUCATION CONSULTANT Kathleen P. Miller

PREPRESS BY Pixel Graphics, Inc.

For Tricia

Molly Dingles

is the author of *Jinka Jinka Jelly Bean* and *Little Lee Lee's Birthday Bang*. As Judy Zocchi, she has written the *Paulie & Sasha* series. She is a writer and lyricist who holds a bachelor's degree in fine arts/theater from Mount Saint Mary's College and a master's degree in educational theater from New York University. She lives in Manasquan, New Jersey, with her husband, David.

Walter Velez

was born in New York. He attended the High School of Art and Design and later the School of Visual Arts. He has done illustration work for many major book and gaming companies. He is known for the popular series *Thieves World* as well as the *Myth* series for Ace Books. He has also produced trading cards for *Goosebumps* and *Dune*. In addition, Walter has illustrated several *Star Wars* books for Random House. He lives in Queens, New York, with his wife, Kriti, and daughter, Kassandra.

The Community of Color series is more than just a series of books about colors. The series demonstrates how individual people, places, and things combine to form a community. It allows children to view the world in segments and then experience the wonderment and value of the community as a whole.

White as a seashell

Blanco como una
concha marina

White sail on a boat

Vela blanca **en un bote**

White as a cloud

Blanco como una nube

White tube set afloat

Tubo blanco puesto a flote

White as a seagull

Blanco como
una gaviota

White robe on a rack

Bata blanca en un perchero

White sailor's hat

Gorro blanco del marinero

White lifeboat in back

Bote salvavidas blanco por detrás

White as a towel

Blanco como una toalla

**White deck shoes
to wear**

**Zapatos marineros
blancos para llevar**

White as a rope

Blanco como una cuerda

White
sea captain's chair

Asiento blanco
del capitán de navío

The color White
is all around.

El color Blanco
está en todas partes.

ABOUT COLOR

Use the Community of Color series to teach your child to identify the most basic colors and to help him or her relate these colors to objects in the real world. ASK:

- What color is this book about?
- Can you name the white things on this boat?
- Can you find a white seashell in this picture?
- What white bird is in this picture?

ABOUT COMMUNITY

Use the Community of Color series to teach your child how he or she is an important part of the community. Explain to your child what a community is.

- A community is a place where people live, work, and play together.
- Your family is a community.
- Your school is a community.
- Your neighborhood is a community.
- The world is one big community.

Everyone plays an important part in making a community work - moms, dads, boys, girls, police officers, firefighters, teachers, mail carriers, garbage collectors, store clerks, and even animals are all important parts of a community. USE THESE QUESTIONS TO FURTHER THE CONVERSATION:

- How are the people on this boat interacting with one another?
- How are the people different from one another? How are they the same?
- What do they have in common?
- How is the community you see in this book like your community? How is it different?
- Describe your community.

ABOUT FEELINGS

Colors can describe as well as evoke different emotions. Encourage your child to describe the feelings that the color white inspires.

- How does the color white make you feel?
- Name your favorite white thing in this book. Why is it your favorite?
- Name your favorite white thing at home. Why is it your favorite?
- Can you tell how the people in the picture feel by looking at their faces?
  Do you ever feel the same way? When? Why?

TRY SOMETHING NEW... Picture time! Use white seashells and pebbles to make and decorate a picture frame. Donate it to the maternity ward in your local hospital.